discovermore

Space Science

Exploring Planets

Elizabeth Pruet

Britannica Educational Publishing

IN ASSOCIATION WITH

THE ROSEN PUBLISHING GROUP

Published in 2026 by Britannica Educational Publishing (a trademark of Encyclopædia Britannica, Inc.) in association with The Rosen Publishing Group, Inc.
2544 Clinton Street, Buffalo, NY 14224

Distributed exclusively by Rosen Publishing.
To see additional Britannica Educational Publishing titles, go to rosenpublishing.com.

Editor: Danielle Haynes
Book Design: Michael Flynn

Photo Credits: Cover Andrey Yurlov/Shutterstock.com; (series background) Dai Yim/Shutterstock.com; pp. 4, 10, 11, 17 (bottom), 20, 22, 23, 25, 26, 27, 29 (top and bottom) courtesy of NASA; p. 5 Jemastock/Shutterstock.com; pp. 6–7 Natalllenka.m/Shutterstock.com; p. 8 Pike-28/Shutterstock.com; p. 9 https://commons.wikimedia.org/wiki/File:The_Mysterious_Case_of_the_Disappearing_Dust.jpg; p. 12 https://commons.m.wikimedia.org/wiki/File:Massive_Smash-Up_at_Vega.jpg; p. 13 BEST-BACKGROUNDS/Shutterstock.com; p. 15 John David Bigl III/Shutterstock.com; p. 17 (top) Angela Cini/Shutterstock.com; p. 19 grayjay/Shutterstock.com; p. 21 https://en.wikipedia.org/wiki/File:Garni_crater_Mars_HiRISE_Sep2015.jpg;

Cataloging-in-Publication Data
Names: Pruet, Elizabeth.
Title: Exploring planets / Elizabeth Pruet.
Description: New York : Britannica Educational Publishing, in association with Rosen Educational Services, 2026. | Series: Discover more: space science | Includes glossary and index.
Identifiers: ISBN 9781641905336 (library bound) | ISBN 9781641905329 (pbk) | ISBN 9781641905343 (ebook)
Subjects: LCSH: Planets--Juvenile literature.
Classification: LCC QB602.P78 2026 | DDC 523.4--dc23

Manufactured in the United States of America

Contents

Planet Basics

As you likely know, Earth is a planet. The word "planet" comes from the Greek word *planetes*, which means "wanderer." Planets are large natural objects that orbit, or travel around, stars. Eight planets orbit the star called the sun. In order from the closest to the sun, these planets are Mercury, Venus, Earth, Mars, Jupiter, Saturn, Uranus, and Neptune. The solar system is the collection of the sun and the objects that orbit around it, including the eight planets.

Saturn, seen here with a few of its moons in 1980, is best known for its large rings of space debris.

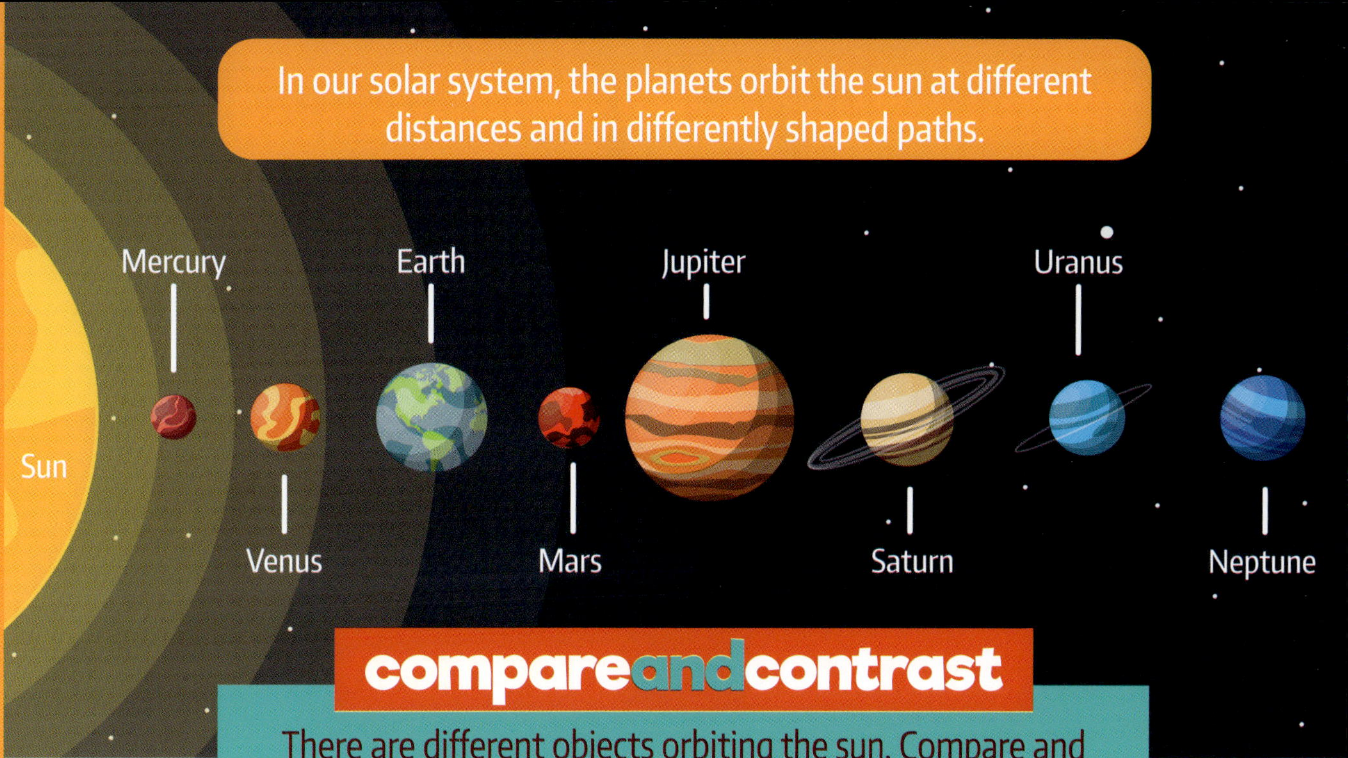

compare and contrast

There are different objects orbiting the sun. Compare and contrast planets, comets, and meteors.

Planets differ from other objects such as comets, asteroids, and meteors. In general, planets are the largest objects in the solar system after the sun. Most of them orbit the sun in a path shaped nearly like a circle. Many also have a layer of gas surrounding them. Most of the planets have at least one moon. Saturn has the most confirmed moons in our solar system—274!

Kinds of Planets

Not all planets are the same. There are two main types in the solar system. The four planets nearest the sun—Mercury, Venus, Earth, and Mars—are called inner planets. They are also called the Earth-like planets. The inner planets are rocky and about the size of Earth or somewhat smaller. They each have solid surfaces. None of these planets has rings, and only Earth and Mars have moons.

The inner planets—Mercury, Venus, Earth, and Mars—are also known as terrestrial planets. Terrestrial refers to the fact that they have solid surfaces.

The gas and ice giants are collectively known as the outer planets.

Jupiter and Saturn are called gas giants, while Uranus and Neptune are ice giants. They are made up mostly of gases. They are all much larger than Earth. Each of the four has a large **atmosphere**. Also, the gas giants each have many moons and a system of rings. Saturn's rings are the largest and best known. Though mostly made of gases, each of the outer planets has a core made of rock and metal.

WORD WISE

AN ATMOSPHERE IS A LAYER OF GASES SURROUNDING A PLANET.

Forming New Planets

It may be hard to believe, but new planets and stars are being formed in the universe all the time. Most scientists believe our solar system began to develop about 4.6 billion years ago. It probably started as a loose cloud of gas and dust. Scientists think that a force called gravity pulled parts of the cloud together into clumps. The clumps squeezed so tightly together that they became hot. The cloud, called the solar nebula, changed shape into a spinning disk and grew even hotter.

Messier 16, commonly known as the Eagle Nebula, is known for being a place where many stars and planets are being formed. Scientists call it a "star nursery."

This is an artist's drawing of a planet-forming disk, with the bright center being the central star.

The largest clump eventually became the sun. The planets developed from the remaining material of the cloud. The disk then began to cool down. Gases in the disk combined into solid objects. The solid objects combined into bigger objects and attracted more material in a process called accretion. Over time, much of the material clumped together into larger bodies called planetesimals. They eventually formed even larger bodies, which, in turn, developed into planets. It's thought that planets take millions of years to form, but new research shows that gas giants could form in as little as 1 million years.

It's hard to know exactly how planets form since it takes millions of years. Scientists developed theories about the formation of the planets based on observations of the solar system. The interior of the solar nebula—a giant cloud of gas and dust—had hotter temperatures near the sun than farther away from the center. Metals and rocks formed from the original cloud of gas and dust. These metal and rock objects formed the inner, rocky planets.

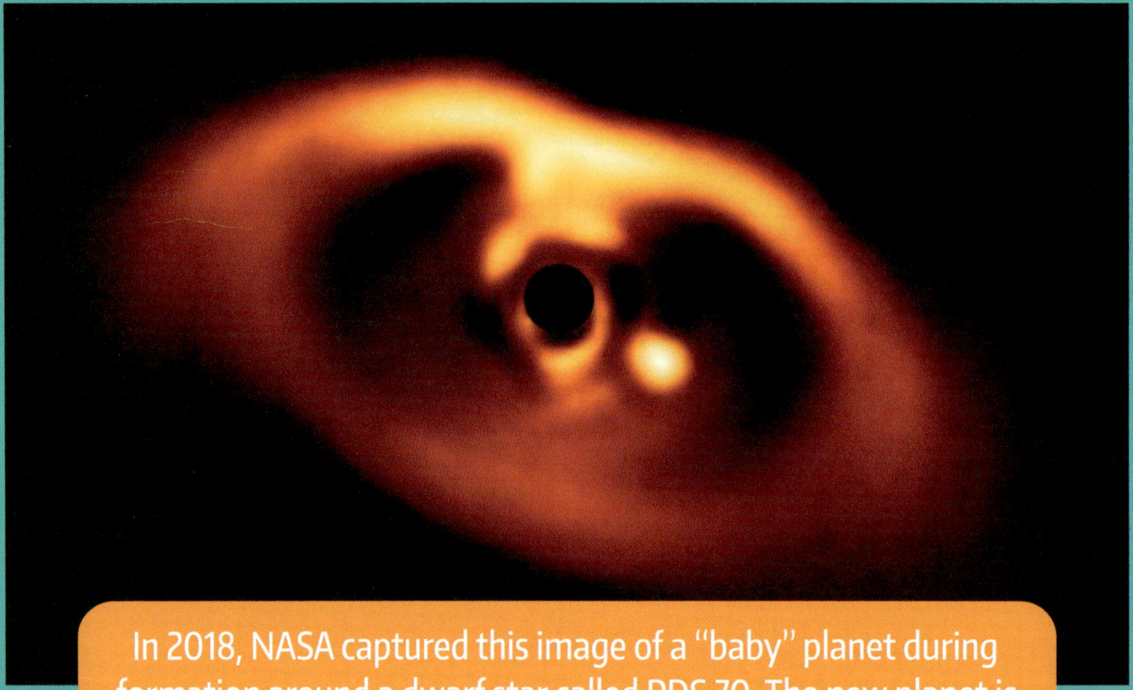

In 2018, NASA captured this image of a "baby" planet during formation around a dwarf star called PDS 70. The new planet is the bright blob to the right of the black circle in the center.

We don't call other planetary systems—such as this one around the star TRAPPIST-1—a "solar system" because "solar" describes only our sun.

Farther away from the hot center near the sun, temperatures were cold enough for ice to form. The ice in the outer planets is made of substances such as water, carbon dioxide, and ammonia. The outer planets grew bigger because of the ice and attracted light elements like hydrogen and helium. These are the most common elements in the universe, so the outer planets were able to grow to large sizes. Once planets have formed and orbit a star, the group is known as a planetary system.

Consider This

The disk of gas spinning around the still-developing sun formed the planets. Why do the planets in our solar system orbit in the same direction?

Violent Creation

The early solar system looked a lot different than it does now. It began when a giant cloud of gas and dust collapsed and began spinning and getting hotter. The planets began as planetesimals. Then they grew into **protoplanets**. The early solar system was very violent. Planetesimals and other forming planets collided with each other. Scientists believe the moon was made when a large piece of Earth broke off after hitting another planetesimal or other object.

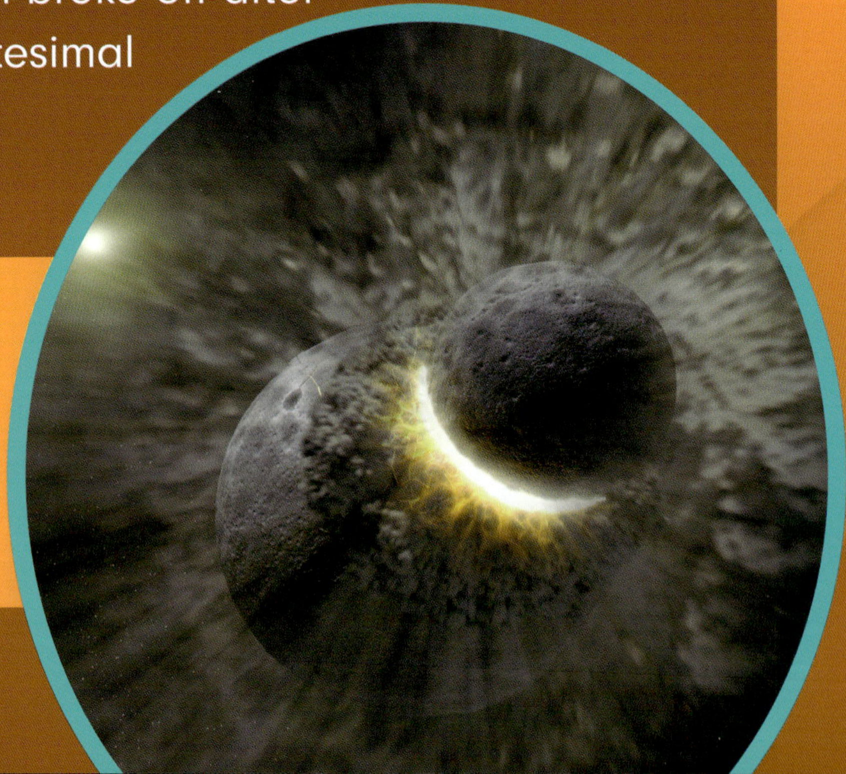

Scientists have found that the rocks on the moon are like those on Earth. This supports the idea that the moon formed after an impact on Earth.

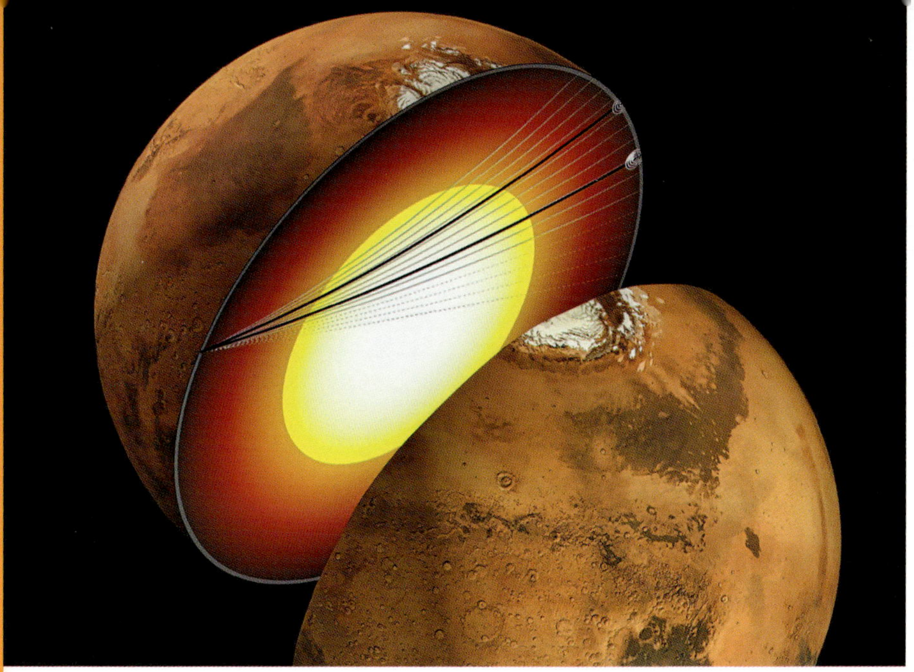

Studying earthquakes on Mars helped scientists learn about the size and composition of the planet's core.

Protoplanets combined with other pieces of matter floating in space and grew bigger. The interiors grew hot and melted. Heavier rocks sank to the center of planets, and lighter rocks were pushed upward. This is called differentiation. These lighter rocks formed the crusts of planets, like the outer part of Earth. Lighter elements such as hydrogen, helium, and oxygen became atmospheres or oceans. Atmospheres change over time; Mars's atmosphere used to be much thicker.

WORD WISE

PROTOPLANETS WERE MOON-SIZED OR LARGER CLUMPS OF MATERIAL THAT BECAME THE PLANETS WE SEE TODAY.

Revolution

Planets in the solar system both rotate and revolve. When they revolve, they orbit the sun, and when they rotate, they spin on their axes (plural of "axis"). So, they each spin like a top while also circling the sun. The path each planet travels around the sun is called an orbit. The eight planets orbit the sun in the same direction as the sun's rotation. The planets' orbits trace a large disk around the sun's equator. Mercury's orbit is the most tilted.

The planets' orbits are not perfect circles. They are slightly oval. The orbits form a type of closed curve called an ellipse. Mercury has the most eccentric, or least circular, orbit of the planets. Venus and Neptune have the most circular orbits. Planets move faster when their orbits bring them closer to the sun and more slowly when they are farther away. The dwarf planet Pluto actually crosses Neptune's orbit, though they never crash into each other.

compare and contrast

Circles and ellipses are different kinds of closed curves. Compare and contrast circles, ellipses, and other closed shapes.

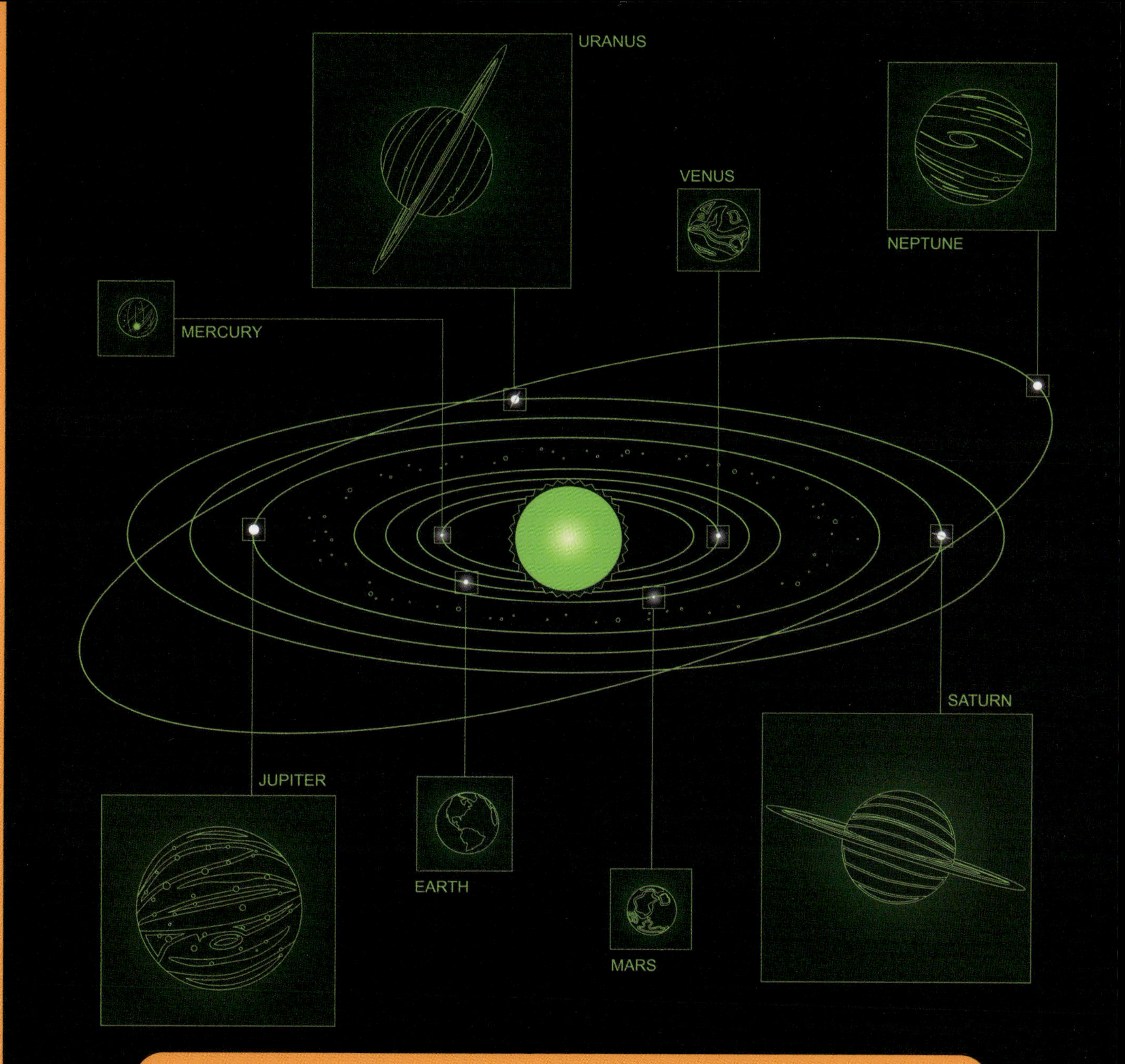

Since the planets each have unique orbits, they're found in different spots in the night sky depending on Earth's own position.

Rotation

While orbiting the sun, each of the planets in our solar system also rotate, or spin on their axes. Most of the planets rotate in the same direction in which they orbit the sun. Only Venus and Uranus rotate in the opposite direction, which is called retrograde rotation. As planets spin, their different sides rotate toward the sun (daytime) and then away from the sun (nighttime).

Mercury and Venus are different because they spin on their axes slowly. By the time they each complete one rotation, they have traveled very far in their orbit around the sun. In fact, a day (the time it takes to spin around once on the axis) on Venus is longer than a year (the time it takes to orbit once around the sun) on Venus. One day on Mercury lasts roughly two-thirds of a year, while there is only about one day in the year on Venus. A day on Venus lasts about 243 Earth days.

Each planet's axis is tilted at a slightly different angle. Uranus's tilt is so extreme, it appears to rotate sideways.

compare and contrast

The length of a day on a planet depends on how fast it rotates. If Earth rotated faster, how would the length of a day on Earth change?

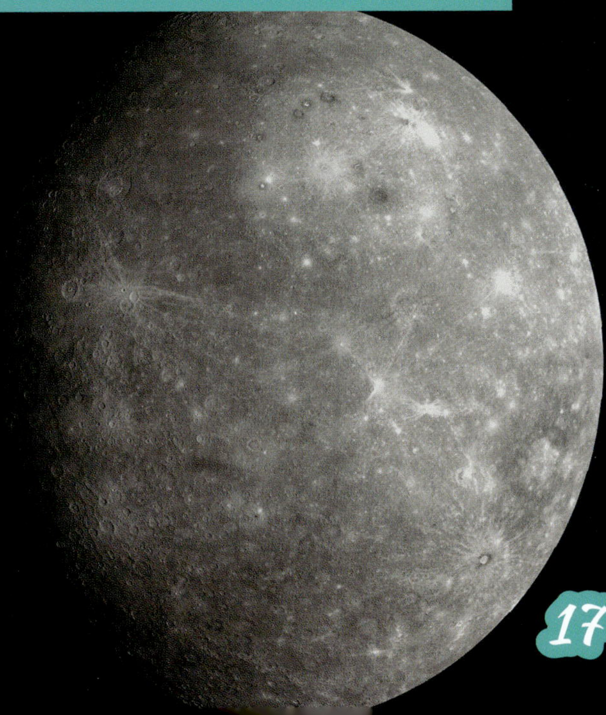

Because of Mercury's unusual path around the sun and slow rotation, its surface temperature varies greatly.

Seasons

Earth isn't the only planet that has seasons. As a planet spins, it turns different portions of its surface toward and then away from the sun. In one day, a person on the planet would seem to see the sun rise, travel overhead, set, and then rise again. A day is equal to the time it takes the planet to complete one rotation. The length of a day is different on every planet. Earth completes one rotation in about 24 hours.

The time it takes a planet to complete one orbit around the sun is equal to a year on that planet. For example, Earth completes one orbit every 365 days, so that is how long a year on Earth lasts. Seasons are caused mainly by the tilt of a planet toward the sun. Mercury, Venus, and Jupiter are barely tilted, so they experience little or no seasonal differences in weather. On planets that do have a tilt, such as Earth, the Northern and Southern Hemispheres experience opposite seasons during the year.

PLANET	DAY LENGTH	YEAR LENGTH
MERCURY	1,408 HOURS	88 DAYS
VENUS	5,832 HOURS	225 DAYS
EARTH	24 HOURS	365 DAYS
MARS	25 HOURS	687 DAYS
JUPITER	10 HOURS	4,333 DAYS
SATURN	11 HOURS	10,759 DAYS
URANUS	17 HOURS	30,687 DAYS
NEPTUNE	16 HOURS	60,190 DAYS

compare and contrast

A year is equal to one complete orbit of a planet around the sun. Compare and contrast the years of the eight planets in the solar system.

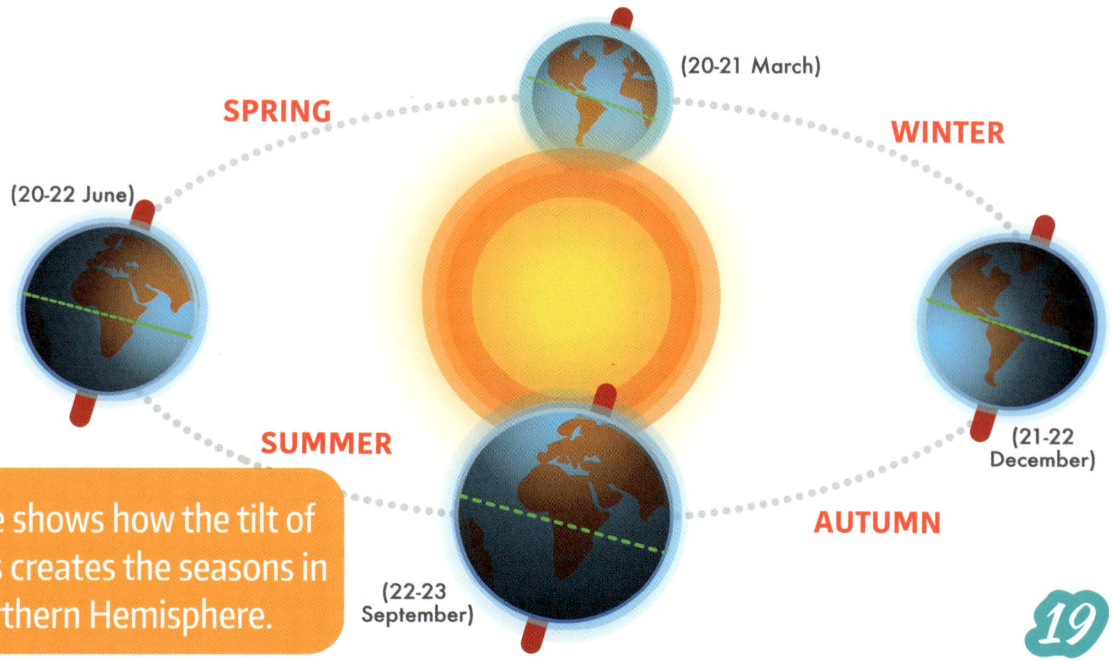

This image shows how the tilt of Earth's axis creates the seasons in the Northern Hemisphere.

The Terrestrial Planets

The four inner—or terrestrial—planets each have rocky surfaces. Mercury is the smallest planet, and it is the closest planet to the sun. It travels around the sun at a faster speed than any other planet. Mercury is very heavy for its size. Venus is Earth's nearest neighbor. Thick clouds always cover the planet. The gases and clouds trap heat. Venus is the hottest planet in the solar system. Venus is about the same size and weight as Earth.

Venus has a thick atmosphere that traps heat, making it hot enough to melt lead on the surface.

These streaks on the wall of a crater on Mars are evidence that water once flowed on the planet's surface.

Earth is the only planet in the solar system that can support life because it has water on its surface and oxygen gas in its air. Earth also has the perfect **range** of temperatures for life. Mars is Earth's outer neighbor. Water exists on Mars as ice caps and patches of ice beneath its surface. Scientists are trying to find out if very tiny, simple life-forms may have ever existed on Mars. NASA wants to send astronauts to Mars to help with this search.

WORD WISE

A RANGE IS AN AREA DEFINED BY AN UPPER AND LOWER LIMIT.

The Gas Giants

The outer four planets of our solar system are called gas or ice giants. Of those, Jupiter and Saturn are gas giants. Jupiter consists almost entirely of gases, mainly hydrogen and helium. In terms of volume, it could contain more than 1,300 Earths. The planet has no solid surface. Jupiter's clouds appear in colored spots and bright and dark stripes. One of the spots is a huge storm called the Great Red Spot. The storm is more than twice as wide as Earth. It is believed to have formed more than 300 years ago and may be permanent.

This image of Jupiter shows its Great Red Spot in the bottom-right corner and bright auroras at its north pole.

Saturn's rings make it one of the most unique planets in our solar system.

Saturn is the second-largest planet in the solar system, after Jupiter. However, Saturn is very light for its size. It would float if placed in water. Saturn's center is probably a hot, rocky core. It is known for its beautiful rings. The rings extend thousands of miles out from the planet. They are made up mostly of pieces of rock, ice, and dust, some as small as a grain of sand, others as big as a mountain.

The Ice Giants and Pluto

The two outermost planets in the solar system—Uranus and Neptune—used to be considered gas giants. They were reclassified as ice giants in the second half of the 20th century.

Uranus was the first planet to be discovered after the invention of the telescope. Narrow rings surround Uranus. The rings may be made of ice particles coated with some silicates or carbon-based material that give them a dark and reddish hue.

Neptune is a stormy world. The planet has the highest winds ever discovered in the solar system. The winds are almost supersonic, meaning they are almost faster than the speed of sound. The planet has no solid surface. Scientists think that Neptune has hot, thick liquids deep inside it.

Astronomers got their first up-close look at Pluto in 2015 when NASA's New Horizons spacecraft passed by.

Scientists used to call Pluto the ninth planet. Pluto is a planet-like object that is usually situated beyond Neptune. Pluto is much smaller than the eight planets. In 2006, a group of scientists decided to make a new category for Pluto and similar objects in the solar system. They called the objects dwarf planets. The dwarf planets in our solar system are Ceres, Eris, Haumea, Makemake, and Pluto.

Consider This

Saturn, Uranus, and Neptune have rings. What would a person see in the sky if Earth had rings?

Exoplanets

In the 1990s, scientists began to discover planets outside the solar system called **exoplanets**. These planets orbit around stars other than the sun. It is difficult to know much about such planets because they are so far away. Scientists can find them by looking for certain tiny changes in the position of stars and the light they emit. These changes occur when a planet orbits its star. The gravitational pull of an orbiting planet will cause a star to move in its own very small orbit. And when a planet crosses in front of its star, it dims the observable light that the star emits.

The exoplanet WASP-18b has about 10 times the mass of Jupiter and orbits its star so fast, a year lasts only 23 hours.

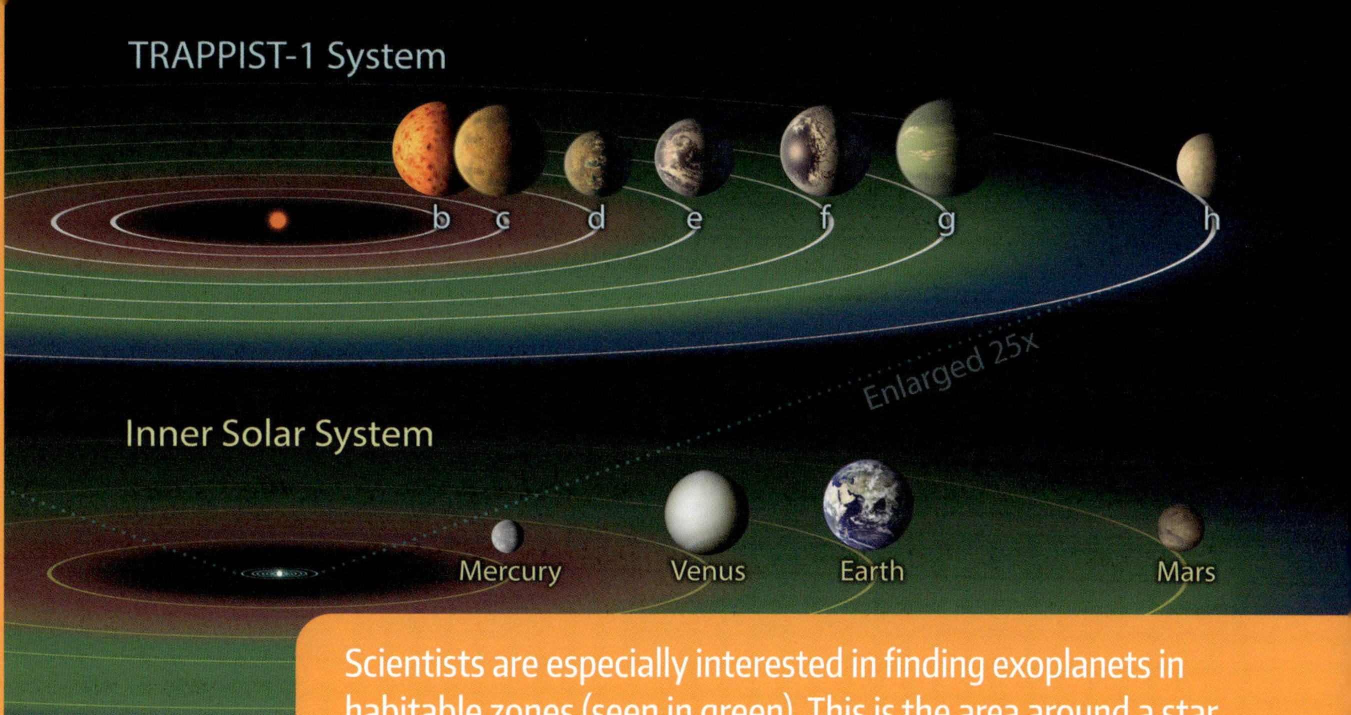

Scientists are especially interested in finding exoplanets in habitable zones (seen in green). This is the area around a star where a planet is likely to have liquid water, the makings for life.

In planetary systems beyond our own, one or more planets orbit a star—just as the eight planets in our solar system orbit the sun. These planets are called exoplanets. Finding other planetary systems is not easy, however, because exoplanets appear much dimmer than the stars they orbit. As space telescopes become more sensitive, they are likely to discover more extrasolar planets. As of mid-2025, astronomers have found nearly 6,000 exoplanets.

WORD WISE

EXOPLANETS MEANS PLANETS OUTSIDE OF OUR SOLAR SYSTEM.

Countless Planets

We don't know exactly how many planets are in our galaxy, the Milky Way, much less the universe. All across the universe, large clouds of dust clumped together and formed planetary systems. Planets formed from these clumps. The planets were of many different types, such as small and rocky or large and made of gas. Today, planets rotate at different speeds and can orbit stars for different lengths of time.

Our solar system is only a small part of a huge system of stars and other objects called the Milky Way galaxy. The Milky Way is just one of billions of other galaxies that make up the universe. There are billions of stars in the universe, and there are even more planets orbiting them. Earth is just one of billions and billions of planets in the sky. How many do you think humans could live on?

This is a drawing of what scientists think the Milky Way galaxy looks like. NASA thinks there could be 10 billion planets in our galaxy.

compare and contrast

Our four seasons depend upon how Earth is tilted toward and away from the sun. Compare and contrast the weather as Earth tilts toward the sun, then tilts away from the sun.

This photo taken by the Hubble Space Telescope shows countless galaxies, each with countless stars—and maybe planets.

Glossary

aurora Arches of light in the atmosphere of a planet's polar regions caused by flares from its star.

collapse To fall in on oneself.

comet An object made of dust and ice orbiting the sun that may form a "tail" as the ice melts.

composition The general makeup of something.

confirmed Known or proven to be true.

core In astronomy, the center part of a planet or star.

crust The outer layer of a planet.

debris Broken pieces of objects or trash left somewhere.

equator A circle around Earth that is as far from the North Pole as it is from the South Pole and that divides the planet into two equal halves—the Northern and Southern Hemispheres.

hemisphere One half of Earth or other planet.

interior The internal part of a thing.

meteor A small object traveling through space and entering Earth's atmosphere.

nursery A room for children or babies; or a place where animals or plants grow.

For More Information

Books

Humphrey, Natalie. *Learn about Mars!* Buffalo, NY: Enslow Publishing, 2024.

Pierce, Simon. *Planets.* Buffalo, NY: Cavendish Square Publishing, 2024.

Stott, Carole. *Eyewitness: Planets.* New York, NY: DK Publishing, 2023.

Websites

NASA Space Place: Solar System
www.spaceplace.nasa.gov/menu/solar-system
Find answers to all your questions about the planets on this NASA website for kids.

National Geographic Kids: What Is a Planet?
www.kids.nationalgeographic.com/space/article/what-is-a-planet
Watch videos and read more about what makes a planet a planet.

Publisher's note to educators and parents: Our editors have carefully reviewed these websites to ensure that they are suitable for students. Many websites change frequently, however, and we cannot guarantee that a site's future contents will continue to meet our high standards of quality and educational value. Be advised that students should be closely supervised whenever they access the internet.

Index